BIBLE STUDIES

Jesus: Listening for His Voice

Kay Arthur & David Arthur

PRECEPT MINISTRIES INTERNATIONAL

WATERBROOK
PRESS

JESUS: LISTENING FOR HIS VOICE

All Scripture quotations are taken from the New American Standard Bible®. Copyright © 1960, 1962, 1963, 1968, 1971, 1972, 1973, 1975, 1977, 1995 by the Lockman Foundation. Used by permission. (www.Lockman.org).

Italics in Scripture quotations reflect the authors' added emphasis.

Trade Paperback ISBN 978-1-60142-808-0
eBook ISBN 978-1-60142-809-7

Copyright © 2015 by Precept Ministries International

Cover design by The Designworks Group

Published in the United States by WaterBrook, an imprint of the Crown Publishing Group, a division of Penguin Random House LLC, New York.

WATERBROOK® and its deer colophon are registered trademarks of Penguin Random House LLC.

Printed in the United States of America
2017

10 9 8 7 6 5 4 3

SPECIAL SALES
Most WaterBrook books are available at special quantity discounts when purchased in bulk by corporations, organizations, and special-interest groups. Custom imprinting or excerpting can also be done to fit special needs. For information, please e-mail specialmarketscms@penguinrandomhouse.com or call 1-800-603-7051.

CONTENTS

HOW TO USE THIS STUDY

This small-group study is for people who are interested in learning for themselves more about what the Bible says on various subjects, but who have only limited time to meet together. It's ideal, for example, for a lunch group at work, an early morning men's group, a young mothers' group meeting in a home, a Sunday-school class, or even family devotions. (It's also ideal for small groups that typically have longer meeting times—such as evening groups or Saturday morning groups—but want to devote only a portion of their time together to actual study, while reserving the rest for prayer, fellowship, or other activities.)

This book is designed so that all the group's participants will complete each lesson's study activities *at the same time*. Discussing your insights drawn from what God says about the subject reveals exciting, life-impacting truths.

Although it's a group study, you'll need a facilitator to lead the study and keep the discussion moving. If *you* are your group's facilitator, the leader, here are some helpful points for making your job easier:

- Go through the lesson and mark the text before you lead the group. This will give you increased familiarity with the material and will enable you to facilitate the group with greater ease. It may be easier for you to lead the group through the instructions for marking if you, as a leader, choose a specific color for each symbol you mark.

- As you lead the group, start at the beginning of the text and simply read it aloud in the order it appears in the lesson, including the Insight boxes that appear throughout. Work through the lesson together, observing and discussing what you learn. As you read the Scripture verses, have the group say aloud the word they are marking in the text.

- The discussion questions are there simply to help you cover the material. As the class moves into the discussion, many times you will find that they will cover the questions on their own. Remember, the discussion questions are there to guide the group through the topic, not to squelch discussion.

- Remember how important it is for people to verbalize their answers and discoveries. This greatly strengthens their personal understanding of each week's lesson. Try to ensure that everyone has plenty of opportunity to contribute to each week's discussions.

- Keep the discussion moving. This may mean spending more time on some parts of the study than on others. If necessary, you should feel free to spread out a lesson over more than one session. However, remember that you don't want to slow the pace too much. It's much better to leave everyone wanting more than to have people dropping out because of declining interest.

- If the validity or accuracy of some of the answers seems questionable, you can gently and cheerfully remind the group to stay focused on the truth of the Scriptures. Your object is to learn what the Bible says, not to engage in human philosophy. Simply stick with the Scriptures and give God the opportunity to speak. His Word *is* truth (John 17:17)!

JESUS: LISTENING FOR HIS VOICE

O ne of the leading causes of both societal and personal demise is the absence of the knowledge and fear of God. To fear God is to discover who He says He is and then to live your life according to that knowledge—respecting, reverencing, trusting the God of all truth. To live in the fear of God is to live according to God's precepts, by His rules, not ours! It is also to realize that consequences are inevitable when we don't value His standards above our own.

In the first of our three studies in the gospel of Mark, *Jesus: Experiencing His Touch,* we considered what happened when Jesus touched people from all walks of life: fishermen, tax collectors, the lame, blind, sick, hungry, and even demon possessed. In each circumstance, the people Jesus came in contact with either believed and reaped the reward of faith, or they resisted the truth and wanted to destroy the One who Mark clearly has told us is the Christ (Messiah), the Son of God and the Son of Man.

Although the touch of Jesus holds the power to heal and transform, only those who believed found their lives truly changed. As they aligned themselves with the One who is truth, they experienced not only miracles but a new and deeper understanding of God. And with that understanding came respect, trust, and a changed life.

Jesus said that man is to live by every word that comes from the mouth of God (Matthew 4:4), so listening, hearing, and believing is imperative. As we study Mark chapters 7–13 in the weeks ahead, we will observe carefully not only what Jesus did, but also what He said. In doing so, may you experience for yourself the freedom and the power that come from knowing truth and living accordingly.

"Tradition!" In the Broadway musical *Fiddler on the Roof*, the main character, Tevye, tries to steer his daughters safely through the shaky ground of a changing world by clinging to tradition—doing things as they'd always been done, remaining faithful to the customs and beliefs of the generations that had gone before.

Have you ever seen the traditions of man make people blind and deaf to truth, prejudiced toward that which holds them captive—when if they would only listen, they could be set free from deception and its destructive consequences?

Let's see what happened when the Son of Man encountered the criticism of the scribes and Pharisees because of tradition!

As you begin your study why don't you ask God to give you ears to hear, to humbly listen to the One sent by God to rescue you from the lie of Satan, who said we can be like God and decide for ourselves what is good and what is evil!

OBSERVE

Leader: Read Mark 7:1–8 aloud, and then read the Insight box on the next page, which gives further information on the scribes and Pharisees.

MARK 7:1–8

1 The Pharisees and some of the scribes gathered around Him when they had come from Jerusalem,

2 and had seen that some of His disciples were eating their bread

with impure hands, that is, unwashed.

3 (For the Pharisees and all the Jews do not eat unless they carefully wash their hands, thus observing the traditions of the elders;

4 and when they come from the market place, they do not eat unless they cleanse themselves; and there are many other things which they have received in order to observe, such as the washing of cups and pitchers and copper pots.)

5 The Pharisees and the scribes asked Him, "Why do Your disciples not walk according to the tradition of

INSIGHT

Scribes were skilled writers, often trained in the Word of God and thus considered experts in the Law and interpreting it. Known also as teachers of the Law, many scribes were of the sect of the Pharisees.

Pharisee means "separated one." Their lives were devoted to the Torah, the first five books of the Bible written by Moses and often referred to as the Law. Because of their devotion, they stressed separation from the strong influence of the classical Greek culture. As the religious (and often political) leaders of the people, they assumed the responsibility for interpreting how the Law was to be lived out in the culture of the times. In their thinking, obedience to the Law was the way to God. Consequently, the Pharisees became teachers of a twofold law: the written Law and oral tradition. The oral tradition was their interpretation of the written Law.

Leader: *Read Mark 7:1–8 aloud again.*
Have the group do the following:
- *Mark with a big* **P** *all the references to*
  the Pharisees, scribes, *and* **the Jews,**
  including pronouns.
- *Mark every reference to* **Jesus** *with a*
  cross:✝ In the same way, mark any
  synonyms and pronouns that refer to
  Jesus Christ. Since you'll be marking re-
  ferences to Jesus so often, you may prefer
  to use a particular color to mark the ref-
  erences to Him so they pop on the page.
- *Put a tall box over all references to* **tra-**
  dition, *like this:* ☐

As you read the text, it's helpful to have the
group say the key words aloud as they mark
them. This way everyone will be sure they are
marking every occurrence of the word,
including any synonymous words or phrases.
Do this throughout the study.

the elders, but eat their bread with impure hands?"

6 And He said to them, "Rightly did Isaiah prophesy of you hypocrites, as it is written: 'This people honors Me with their lips, but their heart is far away from Me.

7 'But in vain do they worship Me, teaching as doctrines the precepts of men.'

8 "Neglecting the commandment of God, you hold to the tradition of men."

DISCUSS
- Look at verses 1–2. What concern did the Pharisees raise?

HIS DISCIPLES WERE EATING WITH IMPURE HANDS

• According to verses 3–4, why did they view this as a problem?

NOT OBSERVING THE TRADITIONS OF THE ELDERS

• What did the Pharisees and the scribes ask Jesus in verse 5?

WHY DO YOUR FOLLOWERS NOT WALK WITH THE TRADITIONS OF THE ELDERS

• What do you learn from marking the Pharisees and scribes in verses 6–8?

THEY WERE HYPOCRITES

• What did Jesus call the Pharisees, and why? What did He identify as the real problem?

NEGLECTING THE COMMANDMENT STICKING TO TRADITIONS

MARK 7:9–13

9 He was also saying to them, "You are experts at setting aside the commandment of God in order to keep your tradition.

10 "For Moses said, 'Honor your father

OBSERVE

Leader: *Read Mark 7:9–13 aloud. Have the group continue to mark the text as before:*

• *Mark all mentions of **Jesus**, including pronouns and synonyms.*

• *Beginning with **them** in verse 9, mark with a big **P** all the references to **the Pharisees, scribes,** and **the Jews,** including pronouns.*

• *Mark **tradition** with a tall box:*

DISCUSS

- How did Jesus describe the Pharisees and scribes in verse 9?

HYPOCRITES OF THE COMMANDMENTS

- In verses 10–11 Jesus contrasted the Word of God (what Moses wrote) with the tradition of the Pharisees. What did Moses say?

HONOR THY FATHER/ MOTHER

- In verses 12–13, what did Jesus identify as the result of following their tradition?

YOU INVALIDATE THE WORD OF GOD

- So what is the lesson for us today?

LIVE THE WORD OF GOD

- Based on this exchange, should we assume all tradition is wrong? How could we answer that question from these words of Jesus? (Hint: Look again at verse 9.)

YES; WE MAKE EXCUSES TO FIT OUR WANTS.

and your mother'; and, 'He who speaks evil of father or mother, is to be put to death';

11 but you say, 'If a man says to his father or his mother, whatever I have that would help you is Corban (that is to say, given to God),'

12 you no longer permit him to do anything for his father or his mother;

13 thus invalidating the word of God by your tradition which you have handed down; and you do many things such as that."

MARK 7:14–23

14 After He called the crowd to Him again, He began saying to them, "Listen to Me, all of you, and understand:

15 there is nothing outside the man which can defile him if it goes into him; but the things which proceed out of the man are what defile the man.

16 ["If anyone has ears to hear, let him hear."]

17 When he had left the crowd and entered the house, His disciples questioned Him about the parable.

18 And He said to them, "Are you so lacking in understand-

OBSERVE

The Pharisees were disturbed to see the disciples of Jesus eating without the ritual washing of their hands! Would this defile them—make them spiritually unclean, tainted? Let's see what Jesus says.

Leader: Read Mark 7:14–23 aloud. Have the group…

- *mark references to **hearing** and **listening** with an ear, like this: ♪ We will do this throughout our study.*
- *put a heart over every reference to **the heart**: ♡*
- *mark **defile** with a slash, like this: ╱*

DISCUSS

- Why did Jesus say tell the crowd, "Listen to Me"? What did He want the crowd to understand?

- What do you learn from marking the word *defile*?

- What are the deeds mentioned in verses 21–22? Where do they originate and what do they do?

ing also? Do you not understand that whatever goes into the man from outside cannot defile him,

19 because it does not go into his heart, but into his stomach, and is eliminated?" (Thus He declared all foods clean.)

20 And He was saying, "That which proceeds out of the man, that is what defiles the man.

21 "For from within, out of the heart of men, proceed the evil thoughts, fornications, thefts, murders, adulteries,

22 deeds of coveting and wickedness, as well as deceit, sensuality,

envy, slander, pride and foolishness.

23 "All these evil things proceed from within and defile the man."

MARK 7:24–30

24 Jesus got up and went away from there to the region of Tyre. And when He had entered a house, He wanted no one to know of it; yet He could not escape notice.

25 But after hearing of Him, a woman whose little daughter had an unclean spirit immediately came and fell at His feet.

26 Now the woman was a Gentile, of the

• In Jewish thinking, the mind and the heart are synonymous. The heart is like the command (control) center of a person. Therefore, when you look at the deeds mentioned in verses 21–23, what step(s) would an individual take to keep from doing these "evil things"?

OBSERVE

Leader: Read Mark 7:24–30 aloud and have the group do the following:

• *Mark all references to **Jesus,** including pronouns.*

• *Mark every reference to **the woman** with a big **W.***

• *Place an ear over each mention of **hearing.***

• *Mark references to **unclean spirits** and **demons** with a pitchfork, like this:*

DISCUSS

• What insight do you gain from verse 24 about Jesus' life? HE DID NOT WANT TO BE SEEN

- What did you learn about this woman? What key details are offered in the text?

SHE WISHED TO CHANGE HIS LIFE

- Why do you think she approached Jesus with her request? SHE BELIEVED HIM TO BE HOLY

- How did Jesus respond to her initially? Why do you think He said this?

LET THE CHILDREN BE SATISFIED FIRST

- How did the woman reply? What happened next? THE DOGS UNDER THE TABLE WILL EAT CRUMBS FROM THE CHILDRENS BREAD

- What truths about Jesus have you learned from His words so far in Mark 7? How can you align your life with these truths?

BE TRUE TO YOUR HEART AND NOT HUMAN TRADITIONS

Syrophoenician race. And she kept asking Him to cast the demon out of her daughter.

27 And He was saying to her, "Let the children be satisfied first, for it is not good to take the children's bread and throw it to the dogs."

28 But she answered and said to Him, "Yes, Lord, but even the dogs under the table feed on the children's crumbs."

29 And He said to her, "Because of this answer go; the demon has gone out of your daughter."

30 And going back to her home, she found the child lying on the bed, the demon having left.

MARK 7:31-37

31 Again He went out from the region of Tyre, and came through Sidon to the Sea of Galilee, within the region of Decapolis.

32 They brought to Him one who was deaf and spoke with difficulty, and they implored Him to lay His hand on him.

33 Jesus took him aside from the crowd, by himself, and put His fingers into his ears, and after spitting, He touched his tongue with the saliva;

34 and looking up to heaven with a deep sigh, He said to him, "Ephphatha!" that is, "Be opened!"

OBSERVE

Leader: Read Mark 7:31-37 aloud and have the group mark...

- *each reference to **Jesus**, including pronouns, as they've done previously.*
- ***deaf** with an ear and a slash, like this:*

DISCUSS

- How is the man described in verse 32?

  DEAF /SPEACH DIFFICULITY

- How did the man get to Jesus?

  THE VILLAGERS BROUGYT HIM

- Briefly describe what Jesus did to the deaf man. PUT FINGERJ IN HIS EARS AND HIM SALIVA ON HIS TONGUE

- This is the first time in the gospel of Mark any mention is made of Jesus healing a deaf person who also had a speech impediment. As you think about it, how might Jesus' actions, as described in verse 33, have helped the deaf man, in the light of his affliction?

• What insight does this give you into the healings Jesus performed? Were they all accomplished in the same way?

BASIC / POWERFUL

NO

• What did the people who witnessed this miracle think about Jesus?

THEY WERE ELATED

• Don't you love hearing the stories of those who were helped by Jesus in various circumstances and various ways, or who were changed because of what they heard? What effect do these testimonies have in your life—and in the lives of others?

35 And his ears were opened, and the impediment of his tongue was removed, and He began speaking plainly.

36 And He gave them orders not to tell anyone; but the more He ordered them, the more widely they continued to proclaim it.

37 They were utterly astonished, saying, "He has done all things well; He makes even the deaf to hear and the mute to speak."

WRAP IT UP

Hundreds of years before Jesus confronted the Pharisees, the prophet Isaiah rightly accused God's people of putting tradition over truth. "This people draw near with their words and honor Me with their lip service, but they remove their hearts far from Me, and their reverence for Me consists of tradition learned by rote" (Isaiah 29:13). Instead of listening to and living by the truth, they taught man-made precepts as if they were the very doctrines of God. By doing this, they exchanged the Word of God—the ultimate truth—for the word of man.

This is the passage Jesus quoted when He and the disciples were called out by the Pharisees for failing to wash prior to eating. In Mark 7:4, the Greek word translated as "wash" is literally "baptize." Pharisees had a tradition of baptizing everything—bodies, cups, pots, and vessels—thus sanctifying them, making them "holy." Some manuscripts include even furniture! "Cleanliness is next to godliness" must have been a motto of this Jewish sect. However, their obsession for being ritually clean caused the Pharisees to miss the point. It didn't matter how clean their bodies were, because their hearts were unclean before the Lord. Just like their fathers before them in Isaiah's time, their hearts were far from God. Uncircumcised. Hardened.

Words, beliefs, traditions shape what we are—but what if we've listened to the wrong words? Embraced beliefs that are not true? Held to traditions passed from generation to generation that are contrary to the Word of God?

What then? It's all vanity! Emptiness! Worthless.

Could it be, dear one, that we are so busy doing life and doing church that we don't take time to get alone with God and hear Him speak to our hearts through His Word?

Or, even if we are not physically deaf like the man Jesus healed, are we spiritually hard of hearing and unable to speak truth? Could it be that the blaring noise of life has deafened us to the still small voice of God?

Or are we deceived because we hear so much from the world and so little from God's Word?

Or could it be that our traditions of religion have kept us from a true relationship with our God? Have we added to or even taken away from what the Bible clearly teaches by following our own traditions?

As you've listened to and watched Jesus in Mark 7, what has God said to you?

"If anyone has ears to hear, let him hear" (Mark 7:16).

Many followed Jesus simply for the dinner and the show! Everywhere He went, exciting events seemed to take place. But what power was behind these wondrous happenings?

Who was this Jesus they had chosen to follow? And what did He expect from them?

What a life-shaping, defining study awaits us this week! You are about to discover the answers to these questions and learn what it truly means to be a follower of Jesus Christ.

OBSERVE

In the first book of our three-part study in the gospel of Mark, *Jesus: Experiencing His Touch,* we read in Mark 6 about Jesus feeding five thousand men (not counting women and children) with only five loaves and two fish, with baskets full left over. Now we're about to study another awesome miracle just two chapters later. As you read, consider not just the events described but also what the words of Jesus reveal that can help you understand Him better.

Leader: Read Mark 8:1–12 aloud. Have the group...

- mark every reference to **Jesus,** including pronouns, as they did last week, with a cross or a color.
- underline with an arrow each mention of **the disciples,** like this: ⟶
- mark **Pharisees** with a big **P.**

MARK 8:1–12

1 In those days, when there was again a large crowd and they had nothing to eat, Jesus called His disciples and said to them,

2 "I feel compassion for the people because they have remained with Me now three days and have nothing to eat.

3 "If I send them away hungry to their homes, they will faint on the way; and some of them have come from a great distance."

4 And His disciples answered Him, "Where will anyone be able to find enough bread here in this desolate place to satisfy these people?"

5 And He was asking them, "How many loaves do you have?" And they said, "Seven."

6 And He directed the people to sit down

DISCUSS

• What do you learn from marking references to Jesus in verses 1–3?

IT REVEALS HIS COMPASSIONATE NATURE.

• What did He say and how did the disciples respond?

THEY NEED TO EAT WHERE WILL WE FIND ENOUGH FOR EVERYONE

• How did Jesus involve the disciples in meeting the needs of the people? What did they do and observe?

THEY SERVED THE PEOPLE

THEY SERVED AND DID NOT RUN OUT; BUT, HAD LEFTOVER.

on the ground; and taking the seven loaves, He gave thanks and broke them, and started giving them to His disciples to serve to them, and they served them to the people.

7 They also had a few small fish; and after He had blessed them, He ordered these to be served as well.

8 And they ate and were satisfied; and they picked up seven large baskets full of what was left over of the broken pieces.

9 About four thousand were there; and He sent them away.

10 And immediately He entered the boat

with His disciples and came to the district of Dalmanutha.

11 The Pharisees came out and began to argue with Him, seeking from Him a sign from heaven, to test Him.

12 Sighing deeply in His spirit, He said, "Why does this generation seek for a sign? Truly I say to you, no sign will be given to this generation."

MARK 8:13–21

13 Leaving them, He again embarked and went away to the other side.

14 And they had forgotten to take bread, and did not have more

• What do you observe about Jesus by listening to His words in this situation? How can this shape your perspective on life today?

JESUS/GOD WILL PROVIDE

TRUST IN THE LORD

OBSERVE

Leader: *Read Mark 8:13–21 aloud. Have the group mark the key words as follows:*

• ***Jesus*** *with a cross or color, as before.*

• ***disciples*** *with an arrow.*

• *the words* ***hear*** *and* ***understand*** *with an ear:* ꀕ

DISCUSS

- Where were Jesus and the disciples headed? What was the focus of their conversation?

THE OTHER SIDE
LEAVEN / BREAD

- What concern did Jesus raise?

WHY WERE THE DISCIPLES DOUBTING

- How did the disciples respond?

DAH!

- Had the disciples really heard what Jesus said in verse 15? Explain your answer.

than one loaf in the boat with them.

15 And He was giving orders to them, saying, "Watch out! Beware of the leaven of the Pharisees and the leaven of Herod."

16 They began to discuss with one another the fact that they had no bread.

17 And Jesus, aware of this, said to them, "Why do you discuss the fact that you have no bread? Do you not yet see or understand? Do you have a hardened heart?

18 "Having eyes, do you not see? And having ears, do you not hear? And do you not remember,

19 when I broke the five loaves for the five thousand, how many baskets full of broken pieces you picked up?" They said to Him, "Twelve."

20 "When I broke the seven for the four thousand, how many large baskets full of broken pieces did you pick up?" And they said to Him, "Seven."

21 And He was saying to them, "Do you not yet understand?"

• So how did Jesus redirect the conversation and their attention in verses 17 to 21?

TESTING THEIR MEMORIES

• What do you think Jesus expected them to understand?

THE PREVIOUS MIRICLE PERFORMED

• Have you ever become caught up in minor issues and missed the big picture of who Jesus is and what He wants to do in your life? If so, briefly describe what happened.

MARK 8:22–26

22 And they came to Bethsaida. And they brought a blind man to Jesus and implored Him to touch him.

OBSERVE

Leader: *Read Mark 8:22–26 aloud.*

• *Have the group mark each reference to* **Jesus** *as they've been doing.*

DISCUSS

• What did Jesus do with the blind man? How does this compare with the healing of the deaf man in Mark 7?

RESTORED HIS SIGHT

ALL THINGS ARE POSSIBLE THROUGH JESUS / GOD

• Why do you think Jesus told the healed man not to enter the village? How does this align with all Mark has told you about Jesus?

HE DIDN'T WANT TO CAUSE A MOB OF GREEDY REQUESTS

23 Taking the blind man by the hand, He brought him out of the village; and after spitting on his eyes and laying His hands on him, He asked him, "Do you see anything?"

24 And he looked up and said, "I see men, for I see them like trees, walking around."

25 Then again He laid His hands on his eyes; and he looked intently and was restored, and began to see everything clearly.

26 And He sent him to his home, saying, "Do not even enter the village."

MARK 8:27–33

²⁷ Jesus went out, along with His disciples, to the villages of Caesarea Philippi; and on the way He questioned His disciples, saying to them, "Who do people say that I am?"

²⁸ They told Him, saying, "John the Baptist; and others say Elijah; but others, one of the prophets."

²⁹ And He continued by questioning them, "But who do you say that I am?" Peter answered and said to Him, "You are the Christ."

³⁰ And He warned them to tell no one about Him.

OBSERVE

Many consider our next segment of scripture a pivotal point in the gospel of Mark. Let's read it and see why.

Leader: Read Mark 8:27–33 aloud. Have the group do the following:
- *Mark each reference to **Jesus**, watching carefully for pronouns and synonyms.*
- *Double underline anything that indicates **where** the action is located.*
- *Mark every reference to **the disciples** with an arrow: ⟶*
- *Circle any indication of* (**time**.)
- *Mark **Satan** with a pitchfork, like this:* ⫫

INSIGHT

Two cities in Israel bear the name Caesarea: Caesarea Maritime on the coast of the Mediterranean Sea and Caesarea Philippi in the north at the foot of Mount Hermon. Caesarea Philippi was built by Herod Philip in honor of Julius Caesar. It was formerly called Paneas (now Banias) as this was the place of the shrine of Pan, a Roman God.

DISCUSS

• What two questions did Jesus ask His disciples? *WHO DO THEY SAY I AM AND WHO DO YOU SAY I AM*

INSIGHT

Christos is the Greek word that parallels the Hebrew word *Masiah* (Messiah). It means "the Anointed One of God."

• How important do you think it is that an individual knows who Jesus is? Explain your answer. *UNDERSTAND THE I AM, ALL ENCOMPASSING POWER / BLESSINGS / FORGIVENESS*

31 And He began to teach them that the Son of Man must ① suffer many things and be rejected ② by the elders and the chief priests and the scribes, and be killed, ③ and after three days ④ rise again.

32 And He was stating the matter plainly. And Peter took Him aside and began to rebuke Him.

33 But turning around and seeing His disciples, He rebuked Peter and said, "Get behind Me, Satan; for you are not setting your mind on God's interests, but man's."

THE SON OF MAN
HE WOULD DIE / AND
RETURN.

• How did Jesus refer to Himself in verse 31? What did He want the disciples to know about His future?

• According to verse 31, what *must* the Son of Man do? Number the sequence of events in the text. The first has been numbered for you. 4

INSIGHT

Son of Man is believed to be a Messianic title taken from Daniel 7:13–14, which describes how "one like a Son of Man," a human being, comes to the Ancient of Days and is given dominion, glory, and a kingdom that all the peoples, nations, and men of every language might serve Him. His is an everlasting kingdom that will not be destroyed nor pass away.

Throughout the Gospels, Jesus repeatedly referred to Himself as the Son of Man. In fact the phrase *Son of Man* is used more than three hundred times in the New Testament, the majority spoken by Jesus.

Mark 8:31 is the second use of the phrase in this gospel. The first occurrence is in Mark 2 when Jesus told His listeners that "the Son of Man has authority on earth to forgive sins" (verse 10) and that He "is Lord of the Sabbath" (verse 28). You will see it more frequently used from this point on in Mark.

When you come across the term, remember that as a man, a human being, Jesus fully understands what it is to live in a body of flesh like ours and yet be without sin!

• How did Jesus address Peter in verse 33, and why? What did Peter want to prevent? How does that relate to the purpose of the Son of Man?

SATAN

THE SEQUENCE OF EVENTS

• Who do you personally believe Jesus is, and why?

HE IS ALL / EVERYTHING

NOTHING IS WITHOUT HIM

MARK 8:34–38

34 And He summoned the crowd with His disciples, and said to them, "If anyone wishes to come after Me, he must deny himself, and take up his cross and follow Me.

35 "For whoever wishes to save his life will lose it, but whoever loses his life for My sake and the gospel's will save it.

36 "For what does it profit a man to gain the whole world, and forfeit his soul?

37 "For what will a man give in exchange for his soul?

38 "For whoever is ashamed of Me and

OBSERVE

Leader: Read Mark 8:34–38 aloud. Have the group…

- *mark all references to **Jesus**, including **Son of Man**.*
- *underline with an arrow each mention of **the disciples**.*
- *underline every reference to **anyone**, including **he, his, man, whoever**.*

DISCUSS

- Whom is Jesus addressing in these verses?

  EVERYONE

- What must a person do if he wants to follow Jesus? *TURN YOUR LIFE OVER TO GOD AND PROFESS JESUS AS SAVIOR*

- How would you explain verses 35–37? What does it mean to lose your life? To forfeit your soul?

  GOD WANTS YOUR SOUL/ BEING. NOT YOUR BODY.

• What do you think it means to be ashamed of Jesus? Of His words?

NOT SPEAK UP FOR JESUS
NOT DEFEND HIS WORD

My words in this adulterous and sinful generation, the Son of Man will also be ashamed of him when He comes in the glory of His Father with the holy angels."

• What will happen to anyone who is ashamed of Jesus?

HE WILL NOT KNOW
YOU IN THE END

• Are these verses true for today, for you? If so, what are you called to do and how would you describe that to another person? Practically, what would it look like in your life? What happens if you ignore that calling?

ABSOLUTELY - WE ARE TO BE DECIPLES
FOR GOD. SPREAD THE GOOD NEWS
YOU WILL SURELY DIE AND NOT BE WITH GOD

WRAP IT UP

What is the most important question a person can answer? It is not "Who do you think you are?" Nor is it "What do you plan to accomplish with your life?"

Jesus asked the most important question of His disciples: "Who do you say that I am?" (Mark 8:29). The answer to this question has eternal consequences. What we think about Jesus determines our destiny. If we believe Jesus is anything other than the promised Messiah, the Christ, then we will spend eternity absent from His Father.

So then, what does it mean for us to declare Jesus is the Christ? Our answer is found in Mark 8:34–35.

Jesus says that to follow Him is to deny yourself and take up your cross. To lose your life for His sake, His cause, and His name is to truly find life—life eternal. We are called to declare Jesus as the Christ and to commit ourselves to following Him, no matter the cost.

So who do *you* say that He is?

There's a difference between hearing what Jesus says and listening carefully to His words.

True listening isn't simply acknowledging and accepting the words of Jesus; it involves belief that results in action, in commitment. It's genuine faith that, according to 1 Peter 1:5, plugs you into the power of God and protects you.

It doesn't matter what comes into your life, Jesus can sustain you in and through every crisis of life. So listen carefully.

OBSERVE

In Mark 8 the disciples finally confessed and believed that Jesus was the Christ, the Anointed One. He told them that the Son of Man would suffer, die, and be raised from the dead. But there was more: the Son of Man would come again in the glory of His Father.

Watch now what Mark tells us in chapter 9. Jesus is still speaking to the disciples and the crowd gathered around them. Let's listen with ears to hear.

Leader: *Read Mark 9:1–8 aloud. Have the group do the following:*

MARK 9:1–8

¹ And Jesus was saying to them, "Truly I say to you, there are some of those who are standing here who will not taste death until they see the kingdom of God after it has come with power."

² Six days later, Jesus took with Him Peter and James and John, and brought them up on a high mountain

by themselves. And He was transfigured before them;

3 and His garments became radiant and exceedingly white, as no launderer on earth can whiten them.

4 Elijah appeared to them along with Moses; and they were talking with Jesus.

5 Peter said to Jesus, "Rabbi, it is good for us to be here; let us make three tabernacles, one for You, and one for Moses, and one for Elijah."

6 For he did not know what to answer; for they became terrified.

• *Mark each reference to **Jesus,** including pronouns and synonyms, as before.*
• *Circle anything that indicates **time** or **the order of events,** including **until, after, then.***
• *Draw a rectangle around each mention of **the kingdom of God,** including the pronoun **it:***
• *Put an ear over **listen.***
• *Mark all references to **Elijah** with a big* **E.**

DISCUSS

• What did Jesus tell His disciples in verse 1 about the kingdom of God?

SOME WILL NOT TASTE DEATH UNTIL THEY REACH THE KINGDOM

• Describe the scene in verses 2–4. What happened, when did it happen, and who was involved? Discuss what you know about each person, with the exception of Jesus.

• What do you learn about Jesus? What did He look like, and whom did He talk to?

• What does this tell you about these individuals?

THEY WERE REVERED

• Whose was the voice from heaven, and what did it say? *GOD! HE TOLD THEM TO LISTEN TO HIS SON*

• What happened when the voice became silent? *EVERONE DISAPPEARED EXCEPT JESUS*

• Who was told to listen to Jesus—and why should they?

PETER, JAMES, JOHN

OBSERVE

Does it seem that Peter, James, and John had just seen the kingdom of God? Moses, who represented the Law, and Elijah, who was the first of the prophets, had talked with Jesus. The three disciples saw it, and they heard it. Jesus was transfigured—changed—right before their eyes! God spoke from heaven; they heard His

---

7 Then a cloud formed, overshadowing them, and a voice came out of the cloud, "This is My beloved Son, listen to Him!"

8 All at once they looked around and saw no one with them anymore, except Jesus alone.

MARK 9:9–13

9 As they were coming down from the mountain, He gave them orders not to relate to anyone what they had seen, until the Son of Man rose from the dead.

10 They seized upon that statement, discussing with one another what rising from the dead meant.

11 They asked Him, saying, "Why is it that the scribes say that Elijah must come first?"

12 And He said to them, "Elijah does first come and restore all things. And yet how is it written of the Son of Man that He will suffer many things and be treated with contempt?

13 "But I say to you that Elijah has indeed come, and they did to him whatever they wished, just as it is written of him."

voice, heard His words: "This is My beloved Son, listen to Him!" (Mark 9:7).

And it happened six days after Jesus told them that some would see the kingdom of God after it had come with power! They were the *some!* Peter later wrote about this event (2 Peter 1:13–18).

So what happened when they came down from the Mount of Transfiguration, as it came to be known?

Leader: Read Mark 9:9–13 aloud. Have the group do the following:
- *Mark all the references to **Jesus**, including **the Son of Man**.*
- *Mark the words **rose** and **rising** with an upward arrow, like this:* ↑
- *Draw a tombstone over **dead**, like this:* ⌂
- *Mark references to **Elijah** with a big **E**.*

DISCUSS
- What did you learn about Elijah from marking the text?

HE WILL BE SENT TO RESTORE THE HEARTS OF THE FATHERS

INSIGHT

Whereas Moses represented the Law, Elijah represented the prophets.

In Malachi, the last book of the Old Testament, we find an exhortation to remember the Law of Moses, God's servant, and a prophecy that God will send Elijah the prophet before the coming of the great and terrible day of the Lord. Elijah's mission would be to restore the hearts of the fathers and the children to one another (Malachi 4:4–6) before God established His kingdom on earth.

The writer of the gospel of Mark indicates that the people were familiar with this prophecy. Remember in Mark 6:14–16; 8:27–28, the people thought Jesus might be either John the Baptist, raised from the dead, or the prophet Elijah.

When Jesus said Elijah had come, it is believed by many that John the Baptist fulfilled Elijah's mission before Herod had him beheaded.

MARK 9:14–29

14 When they came back to the disciples, they saw a large crowd around them, and some scribes arguing with them.

15 Immediately, when the entire crowd saw Him, they were amazed and began running up to greet Him.

16 And He asked them, "What are you discussing with them?"

17 And one of the crowd answered Him, "Teacher, I brought You my son, possessed with a spirit which makes him mute;

18 and whenever it seizes him, it slams him to the ground and he foams at the

OBSERVE

Leader: *Read Mark 9:14–29 slowly. Have the group…*

- *mark each reference to **Jesus.***
- *put a pitchfork over each occurrence of **spirit**, including pronouns.*
- *mark references to **belief** with an open book, like this:* ⌒⌒. *We use a book to symbolize the Word of God; faith comes from hearing the Word of God!*
- *mark references to **unbelief** with a book and mark it through with a slash, like this:* ⌒⌒

DISCUSS

- According to the text, when did this event occur? What had James, Peter, and John seen just before this?

AFTER BEING ON THE MOUNTAIN

• Give a brief overview of what happens in the passage.

THEY FACED THE REALITY THAT THEY WERE UNABLE TO HELP

• This is the last account in Mark of Jesus and the disciples encountering demon possession. Move through the text and discuss what you learned from marking the references to the spirit that possessed this young boy.

→

mouth, and grinds his teeth and stiffens out. I told Your disciples to cast it out, and they could not do it."

19 And He answered them and said, "O unbelieving genera-tion, how long shall I be with you? How long shall I put up with you? Bring him to Me!"

20 They brought the boy to Him. When he saw Him, immediately the spirit threw him into a convulsion, and falling to the ground, he began rolling around and foaming at the mouth.

21 And He asked his father, "How long has this been happening to

him?" And he said, "From childhood.

22 "It has often thrown him both into the fire and into the water to destroy him. But if You can do anything, take pity on us and help us!"

23 And Jesus said to him, "'If You can?' All things are possible to him who believes."

24 Immediately the boy's father cried out and said, "I do believe; help my unbelief."

25 When Jesus saw that a crowd was rapidly gathering, He rebuked the unclean spirit, saying to it, "You deaf and mute spirit, I command you, come out of him and

• What do you learn from the dialogue in verses 22–24, specifically in regard to marking *belief* and *unbelief*? Was this a matter of power or of faith?

THE FATHER WAS UNSURE OF HIS BELIEF JESUS'S POWER AND THE FATHERS FAITH

• In Mark 1 and Mark 6 we are told that Jesus went off on His own to pray. Mark 6 also tells us that Jesus gave the disciples authority to cast out evil spirits, and that they did. Read again in Mark 9:29 Jesus' answer to the disciples when they asked why they couldn't cast out the spirit. What do His words reveal?

THIS SPIRIT CAN ONLY BE REMOVED BY PRAYER

• When we pray, what does it show in respect to our relationship to God? Who are we depending on?

THE POWER OF THE HOLY SPIRIT

• How does this apply to your life today?

IN ALL WAYS

do not enter him again."

26 After crying out and throwing him into terrible convulsions, it came out; and the boy became so much like a corpse that most of them said, "He is dead!"

27 But Jesus took him by the hand and raised him; and he got up.

28 When He came into the house, His disciples began questioning Him privately, "Why could we not drive it out?"

29 And He said to them, "This kind cannot come out by anything but prayer."

MARK 9:30–37

30 From there they went out and began to go through Galilee, and He did not want anyone to know about it.

31 For He was teaching His disciples and telling them, "The Son of Man is to be delivered into the hands of men, and they will kill Him; and when He has been killed, He will rise three days later."

32 But they did not understand this statement, and they were afraid to ask Him.

33 They came to Capernaum; and when He was in the house, He began to question them, "What were you discussing on the way?"

OBSERVE

Leader: *Read Mark 9:30–37 aloud. Have the group do the following:*

- *Mark each mention of **Jesus**, including pronouns and synonyms.*
- *Draw an arrow under each mention of **the disciples.***
- *Mark **kill(ed)** with a tombstone:* ⌂
- *Draw an upward arrow over **rise:*** ↑

DISCUSS

- What was Jesus teaching and telling the disciples?

HOW HE WOULD DIE AND RISE UP THREE DAYS LATER

- Did His disciples understand what Jesus was saying? How did they respond?

NO -- THEY WERE AFRAID TO ASK.

- What were the disciples focused on as they walked with Jesus to Capernaum? And what insight do you get from verse 34 about the subject of their discussion?

THEY WERE FOCUSED ON THEMSELVES.
SELF CENTERED

- So what did the Teacher do?

SET THEM DOWN AND

- What do you learn from this text about wanting to be greater than others?

YOU WILL END UP LAST

- What connection do you see between what Jesus said about greatness and what He said and did in verses 36 and 37?

HE WHO RECEIVES HIM WILL BE RECEIVED BY THE FATHER

- So what would it look like for you to live in light of His words today?

DOING ONLY THOES THINGS PLEASING TO GOD

34 But they kept silent, for on the way they had discussed with one another which of them was the greatest.

35 Sitting down, He called the twelve and said to them, "If anyone wants to be first, he shall be last of all and servant of all."

36 Taking a child, He set him before them, and taking him in His arms, He said to them,

37 "Whoever receives one child like this in My name receives Me; and whoever receives Me does not receive Me, but Him who sent Me."

Mark 9:38–41

38 John said to Him, "Teacher, we saw someone casting out demons in Your name, and we tried to prevent him because he was not following us."

39 But Jesus said, "Do not hinder him, for there is no one who will perform a miracle in My name, and be able soon afterward to speak evil of Me.

40 "For he who is not against us is for us.

41 "For whoever gives you a cup of water to drink because of your name as followers of Christ, truly I say to you, he will not lose his reward."

OBSERVE

Leader: Read Mark 9:38–41 aloud. Have the group…

* mark each mention of **Jesus,** including pronouns and **Christ.**

DISCUSS

• What situation did the disciples bring up in verse 38?

A NON FOLLOWER WAS CASTING OUT DEMONS

• Summarize Jesus' teaching in verses 39–41.

IF YOU ARE DOING GOD'S WILL, YOU WILL BE BLESSED

OBSERVE

Leader: Read Mark 9:42–50 aloud. Have the group...

- *underline every **whoever, your,** and **you.***
- *mark every reference to **being cast into hell** with a downward arrow, like this:*

  ↓

- *mark **stumble** with a big **X.***

DISCUSS

- Where did Jesus direct the conversation in verse 42, and what does this tell you about verses 38–41? Who was still right there with Jesus?

  SALVATION AND SIN

- In the light of this, what do you learn about children and our responsibility to them as followers of Jesus Christ?

  HELP GUIDE THEM TO LEARNING ABOUT SALVATION

- What do you learn from marking *stumble* in verse 42?

  FIX THE PROBLEM AND FIND FORGIVENESS

MARK 9:42–50

42 "Whoever causes one of these little ones who believe to stumble, it would be better for him if, with a heavy millstone hung around his neck, he had been cast into the sea.

43 "If your hand causes you to stumble, cut it off; it is better for you to enter life crippled, than, having your two hands, to go into hell, into the unquenchable fire,

44 [where their worm does not die, and the fire is not quenched.]

45 "If your foot causes you to stumble, cut it off; it is better for you to enter life lame, than, having

your two feet, to be cast into hell,

46 [where their worm does not die, and the fire is not quenched.]

47 "If your eye causes you to stumble, throw it out; it is better for you to enter the kingdom of God with one eye, than, having two eyes, to be cast into hell,

48 where their worm does not die, and the fire is not quenched.

49 "For everyone will be salted with fire.

50 "Salt is good; but if the salt becomes unsalty, with what will you make it salty again? Have salt in yourselves, and be at peace with one another."

- What are some ways a person's hands, feet, and eyes might cause them to stumble?

IN THEIR SINNING NATURE

- What is the consequence of not controlling your hands, your feet, or your eyes? What will you miss, and where will you end up? *YOU WILL MISS SALVATION AND ENTER INTO HELL*

- As you read Jesus' words, does He seem to be talking about hell as a literal place? Explain your answer.

YES

- Do you agree? Do you think you can believe Him? Why or why not?

YES ~ WE HAVE TO HAVE FAITH

- You've observed the words of the Son of God. What would it look like practically for you to listen to and apply these words in your life today?

MY LIFE FALLS WAY SHORT OF PERFECT.

WRAP IT UP

Can you imagine the desperation that gripped the father of the demon-oppressed boy in this lesson? How painful it must have been to watch his poor son convulsing on the ground, enduring years of torment from something he could not see or defend himself against.

Don't you just love the father's honest declaration to Jesus? "I do believe; help my unbelief" (Mark 9:24).

Today, each of us might give the same reply to Jesus' statement, "All things are possible to him who believes" (verse 23). We want to believe the words of Jesus, but we have to fight against our skepticism—and the culture's denigration of a childlike faith.

Believing is the action side of faith. The struggling father believed and asked for help in his unbelief. A few verses later Jesus called for all of us to receive Him like a child, to adopt a simple, single-minded, childlike faith.

You've heard the words that were read this week, but can you say you listened carefully and truly believed?

If you are struggling, why don't you cry out to the One who had these truths written down: "I do believe; help my unbelief." It's a great place to start! His ear is not deaf that it cannot hear, and His arm is not so short that it cannot save (Isaiah 59:1).

If someone were to ask you, "Why did Jesus really come?" what would your answer be? If they asked you what is expected of a follower of Jesus Christ, would you give them a straight answer—the uncompromised truth that it means making God's priorities our own, laying down our own dreams and desires to follow Jesus? Or would you try to soften it to get them to buy in to Christianity?

As you read Mark 10 and study for yourself the words of Jesus, ask God for ears to listen—to truly hear, understand, and live by what He says.

OBSERVE

Leader: Read Mark 10:1–12 aloud. Have the group...

- *mark each reference to **Jesus**.*
- *circle **divorce** and draw an arrow pointing away from it, since the word means "to send away":*
- *put a big **A** over every mention of **adultery**.*

DISCUSS

- What is the situation in this passage? What question did the Pharisees pose to Jesus, and why?

MARK 10:1–12

1 Getting up, He went from there to the region of Judea and beyond the Jordan; crowds gathered around Him again, and, according to His custom, He once more began to teach them.

2 Some Pharisees came up to Jesus, testing Him, and began to question Him whether

it was lawful for a man to divorce a wife.

³ And He answered and said to them, "What did Moses command you?"

⁴ They said, "Moses permitted a man to write a certificate of divorce and send her away."

⁵ But Jesus said to them, "Because of your hardness of heart he wrote you this commandment.

⁶ "But from the beginning of creation, God made them male and female.

⁷ "For this reason a man shall leave his father and mother,

• Look at verses 3–4. How did Jesus respond, and what did that make the questioners do?

THEY ADMITTED THEY KNEW

• Then what did Jesus do in verses 5–9?

YOU CAN DO IT; BUT GOD'S WORD DOES'T WANT YOU TO.

• What can you learn from Jesus' approach that you could apply when anyone challenges or tests your beliefs?

READ GODS WORD FOR DIRECTION

• What did you learn from marking *divorce* and *adultery*?*

THERE IS A LOT OF GUIDENCE AVAIL ON THE SUBJECTS

---

* This is not the full teaching on the subject of divorce and remarriage. If you want to study the subject for yourself from the Word of God, we highly recommend our course on *Marriage Without Regrets*. It is a powerful and thorough study of the entire subject of marriage, including divorce and remarriage, and is available in numerous languages. Go to www.precept .org. We also offer two 40-Minute Studies you might find helpful: *Building a Marriage That Really Works* and *Finding Hope After Divorce*.

8 and the two shall become one flesh; so they are no longer two, but one flesh.

9 "What therefore God has joined together, let no man separate."

10 In the house the disciples began questioning Him about this again.

11 And He said to them, "Whoever divorces his wife and marries another woman commits adultery against her;

12 and if she herself divorces her husband and marries another man, she is committing adultery."

MARK 10:13–16

13 And they were bringing children to Him so that He might touch them; but the disciples rebuked them.

14 But when Jesus saw this, He was indignant and said to them, "Permit the children to come to Me; do not hinder them; for the kingdom of God belongs to such as these.

15 "Truly I say to you, whoever does not receive the kingdom of God like a child will not enter it at all."

16 And He took them in His arms and began blessing them, laying His hands on them.

OBSERVE

Leader: Read Mark 10:13–16 aloud and have the group…

- *mark each reference to **Jesus**.*
- *draw a box around each occurrence of the phrase **the kingdom of God**:* ☐

DISCUSS

- What do you learn about Jesus in this passage? Note carefully what Mark reveals about Jesus' feelings and the way He deals with people. You don't want to miss anything. HE WILL FAVOR CHILDREN

- What did you learn about the kingdom of God? How is it described in these verses? IT IS FOR THE INOCENT OF SIN

- Why does Jesus use the illustration of a child? What qualities of children do you think Jesus had in mind as He described the kingdom of God? LACK OF SIN

OBSERVE

Leader: *Read Mark 10:17–31 aloud and slowly so the group can mark and take in the text in its entirety. Have them…*

- *mark every reference to **Jesus,** including pronouns and synonyms.*
- *underline the references to **the man**.*

Leader: *Read through the text a second time. This is an important segment for the group to understand. Have the group…*

- *draw a box around each occurrence of the phrase **the kingdom of God.***
- *mark every reference to **wealth,** including **rich** and **much property,** with a dollar sign: $*

DISCUSS

- What do you learn about the man who approached Jesus? *HE WAS SINLESS*

- What is the first thing Jesus pointed out to this man in verse 18?
  NO ONE IS GOOD EXCEPT GOD

MARK 10:17–31

17 As He was setting out on a journey, a man ran up to Him and knelt before Him, and asked Him, "Good Teacher, what shall I do to inherit eternal life?"

18 And Jesus said to him, "Why do you call Me good? No one is good except God alone.

19 "You know the commandments, 'Do not murder, Do not commit adultery, Do not steal, Do not bear false witness, Do not defraud, Honor your father and mother.'"

20 And he said to Him, "Teacher, I have kept all these things from my youth up."

21 Looking at him, Jesus felt a love for him and said to him, "One thing you lack: go and sell all you possess and give to the poor, and you will have treasure in heaven; and come, follow Me."

22 But at these words he was saddened, and he went away grieving, for he was one who owned much property.

23 And Jesus, looking around, said to His disciples, "How hard it will be for those who are wealthy to enter the kingdom of God!"

24 The disciples were amazed at His words. But Jesus answered again and said to

- How does this relate to our earlier discussion in week 2 of who Jesus is?

  JESUS IS THE SPIRIT OF GOD

- What can you suppose about the status of the man from verses 22, 23, and 25?

  HE WAS GOD LIKE IN HIS LIFE

- According to verse 21, how did Jesus feel about this man, and what did He want the man to do?

  SELL EVERYTHING AND FOLLOW JESUS

- What kept the man from following Jesus? What does this tell you about the man's priorities?

  HE DID NOT WANT TO BE POOR

- Mark tells us in verse 22 the man walks away. In the light of the man's question to Jesus in verse 17 and what Jesus says in verses 23–25, what do you assume happened to this man—and why?

  HE WAS DENIED

- What do you learn from the text about salvation and entering the kingdom of God?

  YOU CAN'T BUY YOUR WAY IN

- Ultimately, how does salvation come to an individual?

  THROUGH ASKING AND THE GRACE OF GOD

- Verse 28 tells us "Peter began to say." Say what and why? What prompted Peter's words?

them, "Children, how hard it is to enter the kingdom of God!

25 "It is easier for a camel to go through the eye of a needle than for a rich man to enter the kingdom of God."

26 They were even more astonished and said to Him, "Then who can be saved?"

27 Looking at them, Jesus said, "With people it is impossible, but not with God; for all things are possible with God."

28 Peter began to say to Him, "Behold, we have left everything and followed You."

29 Jesus said, "Truly I say to you, there is no one who has left house or brothers or sisters or mother or father or children or farms, for My sake and for the gospel's sake,

30 but that he will receive a hundred times as much now in the present age, houses and brothers and sisters and mothers and children and farms, along with persecutions; and in the age to come, eternal life.

31 "But many who are first will be last, and the last, first."

• And what did Jesus teach the disciples?

WHAT YOU DO IS FOR GOD'S SAKE

• Have you been rejected by your family or suffered loss because of your decision to follow Jesus Christ? How does knowing what Jesus said help—or does it?

KEEP YOUR FAITH

• What are we assured of in verse 30? When will this take place? And how, practically, can knowing this help us in our personal situation?

BE FAITHFUL

• Note that Jesus' promise includes the phrase "along with persecutions." Is this evident today? If so, where and how? Why the persecution?

HE ALLOWS SATAN TO TORMENT US WHEN WE NEED TO WAKE UP

OBSERVE

As you study this next section remember Mark's gospel was written around the time of Peter's martyrdom. Persecution had already been experienced by many of Jesus' followers; therefore, the words of Jesus recorded by Mark could help prepare them for the crisis to come under Nero, the Caesar of Rome.

Leader: Read Mark 10:32–45 aloud. Have the group mark…

- *every reference to **Jesus,** including the phrase **Son of Man.***
- ***rise** with an upward arrow:* ↑
- ***serve(d), slave, servant** with a downward semicircle, like this:* ⌒

DISCUSS

- Where was Jesus headed? What did He do with the Twelve?

TO HIS DEATH
HE TRIED TO ENLIGHTEN
THEM

32 They were on the road going up to Jerusalem, and Jesus was walking on ahead of them; and they were amazed, and those who followed were fearful. And again He took the twelve aside and began to tell them what was going to happen to Him,

33 saying, "Behold, we are going up to Jerusalem, and the Son of Man will be delivered to the chief priests and the scribes; and they will condemn Him to death and will hand Him over to the Gentiles.

34 "They will mock Him and spit on Him, and scourge Him and kill Him, and three days later He will rise again."

35 James and John, the two sons of Zebedee, came up to Jesus, saying, "Teacher, we want You to do for us whatever we ask of You."

36 And He said to them, "What do you want Me to do for you?"

37 They said to Him, "Grant that we may sit, one on Your right and one on Your left, in Your glory."

38 But Jesus said to them, "You do not know what you are asking. Are you able to drink the cup that I drink, or to be

• This is the third time Jesus spoke of His death and resurrection. The preceding two times are recorded in Mark 8:31 and 9:31. In this passage what specifics are given about what will happen to the Son of Man? Why did Jesus want His followers to know this?

VRS 34
IT IS NOT AN EASY
ROAD TO THE KINGDOM

• What purpose might be served by the disciples knowing this?

THEY WILL KNOW WHAT
TO EXPECT AND THEY
CAN PROCLAIM IN THEIR
TEACHING OF HIS RETURN

• What was the response of James and John, men Jesus referred to as "Sons of Thunder" (Mark 3:17)? What does this suggest about how well they were listening to Jesus?

• How did Jesus deal with these Sons of Thunder?

WARNED THEM THEY ARE NOT HERE TO PLEASE JESUS, BUT, TO PLEASE/HONOR GOD

• What was the cup, the baptism that awaited Jesus?

HIS BLOOD

• How did the other ten disciples react to this conversation? Why, from the context, do you think they felt as they did? Was their concern about the impending events Jesus had just described? Were they really listening?

THEY MAY HAVE FELT LIKE THEY WERE ABOUT TO BE JOBLESS

• So what truth did Jesus teach in verses 42–45?

YOU MUST SERVE AND NOT EXPECT TO BE SERVED

baptized with the baptism with which I am baptized?"

39 They said to Him, "We are able." And Jesus said to them, "The cup that I drink you shall drink; and you shall be baptized with the baptism with which I am baptized.

40 "But to sit on My right or on My left, this is not Mine to give; but it is for those for whom it has been prepared."

41 Hearing this, the ten began to feel indignant with James and John.

42 Calling them to Himself, Jesus said to them, "You know that those who are

recognized as rulers of the Gentiles lord it over them; and their great men exercise authority over them.

43 "But it is not this way among you, but whoever wishes to become great among you shall be your servant;

44 and whoever wishes to be first among you shall be slave of all.

45 "For even the Son of Man did not come to be served, but to serve, and to give His life a ransom for many."

• Why did the Son of Man come?

TO TEACH / MAKE DECIPLES AND DIE FOR OUR SINS

• So how could truly listening to these words of Jesus impact the way you live day by day?

YOU REALIZE HOW YOU DO NOT MEASURE UP

OBSERVE

As we study these final seven verses of Mark 10, remember Jesus was on His way to Jerusalem, traveling with a crowd—a crowd that was fearful (verse 32). In all probability they were journeying to Jerusalem not just because of Jesus, but also because it was almost time for the feast of Passover.*

Leader: Read Mark 10:46–52 aloud. Have the group…

- *mark all references to **Jesus**, including **Son of David**.*
- *underline references to **the blind beggar**.*

---

* For more on the Passover, be sure to read the next study in this series, *Jesus: Understanding His Death and Resurrection.*

MARK 10:46–52

46 Then they came to Jericho. And as He was leaving Jericho with His disciples and a large crowd, a blind beggar named Bartimaeus, the son of Timaeus, was sitting by the road.

47 When he heard that it was Jesus the Nazarene, he began to cry out and say, "Jesus, Son of David, have mercy on me!"

48 Many were sternly telling him to be quiet, but he kept crying out all the more, "Son of David, have mercy on me!"

49 And Jesus stopped and said, "Call him here." So they called the blind man, saying to him, "Take courage, stand up! He is calling for you."

50 Throwing aside his cloak, he jumped up and came to Jesus.

51 And answering him, Jesus said, "What do you want Me to do for you?" And the blind man said to Him, "Rabboni, I want to regain my sight!"

52 And Jesus said to him, "Go; your faith has made you well." Immediately he regained his sight and began following Him on the road.

Israel in the Time of Christ

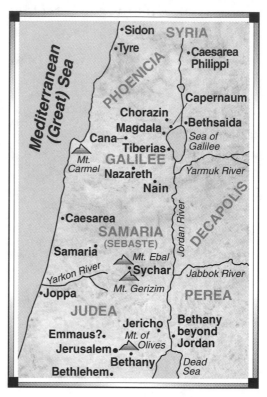

DISCUSS

• What's the focus of these final seven verses? Summarize the 5 *Ws* and an *H*— the who, what, when, where, why, and how—of these verses. *THROUGH FAITH IT IS POSSIBLE*

• What details did Mark include about the blind man? *HE HAD FAITH IN THE SON OF GOD*

- How does this compare with the level of information Mark has given about any other people Jesus healed?

- This is not the first record in Mark of Jesus healing a blind man. So why another account? When the blind man first called out to Jesus, how did he identify Him? What title did he give Jesus? Once or more? What does the text say?

JESUS SON OF DAVID/ RABBONI

- Did Jesus in any way rebuke the blind Bartimaeus for calling Him the Son of David?

NO

• What gave Bartimaeus his sight?

HIS FAITH

• If Jesus asked, "What do you want Me to do for you?" how would you answer?

ALLOW ME TO COME HOME TO YOUR KINGDOM

INSIGHT

Jesus was headed to Jerusalem, the Holy City, where it was prophesied that at "the end of the days" the Son of David would rule as King of kings. This is the first time in the gospel of Mark that Jesus is identified as "Son of David." According to the Old Testament prophecies, the Christ, the Messiah, had to be the Son of David. God had made a covenant with David that his descendent would sit on the throne of Israel forever (2 Samuel 7; Psalm 89).

WRAP IT UP

Throughout the gospel of Mark, we see Jesus spending time with ordinary people, those whom others might even consider unimportant—children, the demon possessed, those who were sick or disabled, who lacked power to help even themselves. His actions and words revealed the upside-down kingdom of God, in which the first shall be last and the last shall be first. The life and ministry of Jesus pointed to the great reversal of power, displacing the world's preconceived notions about societal ranks and what was truly important.

In this week's lesson we saw how Jesus' words to His followers direct us to have childlike faith, to realize that wealth can actually be an impediment to entering the kingdom of God. Through the scene in which Jesus' own disciples jockeyed for position in the kingdom, we learned that to be great we must humble ourselves to serve. And we encountered a blind man who saw Jesus for who He really is, the Son of David—the rightful heir to the throne of Israel, the Anointed One who would establish God's kingdom on earth!

In view of these glimpses of how God's kingdom works, we need to ask ourselves, Do we want to be first or last? Are we guilty of seeking to promote ourselves in the eyes of others? Do we seek to establish our own positions with Jesus, making demands on where we are placed in life, or do we want to follow Jesus in laying down our lives?

May these words of Christ sink deep into our hearts and direct our lives: "Whoever wishes to be first among you shall be slave of all. For even the Son of Man did not come to be served, but to serve" (Mark 10:44–45).

Last week we read about Jesus restoring sight to blind Bartimaeus, who, in faith, called on the Son of David to heal him. As we pick up the story in Mark 11, Bartimaeus is following Jesus into Jerusalem. Although it was a long walk, about twenty-one miles, can you imagine the joy of Bartimaeus as he climbed those hills, undoubtedly singing the Psalms, the Songs of Ascent, and for the first time catching glimpses of the Holy City on the distant Mount Zion?

Bartimaeus was making Aliyah—going up to Jerusalem, where someday the Son of God, the Son of Man, the Son of David, would sit on His glorious throne ruling all the nations of the earth.

Yet before the crown there would be a cross.

Passover was coming. Jesus had come to give His life as a ransom for many, and the Passover Lamb had to be shown to be without spot or blemish.

Let's see who Jesus encountered and how He responded, and let's listen carefully to all He taught in those days lived in the shadow of Golgotha's cross.

MARK 11:1–11

¹ As they approached Jerusalem, at Bethphage and Bethany, near the Mount of Olives, He sent two of His disciples,

² and said to them, "Go into the village opposite you, and immediately as you enter it, you will find a colt tied there, on which no one yet has ever sat; untie it and bring it here.

³ "If anyone says to you, 'Why are you doing this?' you say, 'The Lord has need of it'; and immediately he will send it back here."

⁴ They went away and found a colt tied at the door, outside in

OBSERVE

Leader: Keep in mind that this lesson covers a lot of ground, taking us through Mark 11 into Mark 12. Read Mark 11:1–11 aloud slowly. Have the group…

- *double underline anything that describes a **geographical location** or **physical position**.*
- *mark each reference to **Jesus**.*
- *draw a box around **kingdom:** ☐*

Jerusalem in the Time of Christ

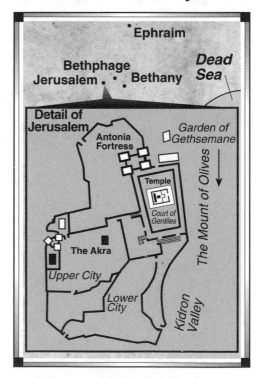

DISCUSS

• Look at the map on the previous page and locate the places named in verses 1–11.

? 11-1
o

• How did the people react when Jesus rode into Jerusalem?

WITH PRAISE/ADORATION

INSIGHT

Hosanna (which means "save us, we pray") simply became a Hallel, which is an expression of praise.

The phrase "Blessed is the one who comes in the name of the LORD" is taken from Psalm 118:26.

When a king rode into a city on a donkey, it was a sign that he was coming for peace; if it was on a white horse, he was coming to conquer.

• What do you learn about the when and the who of the kingdom from verse 10?

TYING THE SON OF DAVID TO THE KINGDOM OF GOD, WHEN JESUS RETURNS.

---

the street; and they untied it.

5 Some of the bystanders were saying to them, "What are you doing, untying the colt?"

6 They spoke to them just as Jesus had told them, and they gave them permission.

7 They brought the colt to Jesus and put their coats on it; and He sat on it.

8 And many spread their coats in the road, and others spread leafy branches which they had cut from the fields.

9 Those who went in front and those who followed were shouting: "Hosanna! Blessed is He who comes in the name of the LORD;

10 Blessed is the coming kingdom of our father David; Hosanna in the highest!"

11 Jesus entered Jerusalem and came into the temple; and after looking around at everything, He left for Bethany with the twelve, since it was already late.

MARK 11:12–19

12 On the next day, when they had left Bethany, He became hungry.

13 Seeing at a distance a fig tree in leaf, He went to see if perhaps He would find anything on it; and

• How does this fit with what Bartimaeus called Jesus back in Jericho?

PARALEL'S THE IDENITY

• What do you learn from verse 11 about Jesus' activities after He entered Jerusalem? Who was with Him?

HE WAS SATISFIED WITH WHAT HE SAW AND TOOK THE 12 DECIPLES ON TO BETHANY

OBSERVE

Leader: *Read Mark 11:12–19 aloud. Have the group do the following:*

• *Mark each reference to **Jesus.***

• *Double underline anything that indicates **location,** including **the temple.***

• *Mark all references to **prayer** like this:* prayer

• *Mark any reference to **teaching** with a big **T.***

INSIGHT

Leaves on fig trees preceded the bearing of fruit. Apparently being hungry and seeing the leaves, Jesus expected fruit.

DISCUSS

• Summarize the events that took place between verses 12 and 19.

JESUS WAS NOT HAPPY WITH WHAT WAS TAKING PLACE IN HIS TEMPLE. SO HE DROVE THEM OUT

• What seemed to be Jesus' reason for cursing this fig tree?

IT HAD NOTHING TO FILL HIS NEED.

when He came to it, He found nothing but leaves, for it was not the season for figs.

14 He said to it, "May no one ever eat fruit from you again!" And His disciples were listening.

15 Then they came to Jerusalem. And He entered the temple and began to drive out those who were buying and selling in the temple, and overturned the tables of the money changers and the seats of those who were selling doves;

16 and He would not permit anyone to carry merchandise through the temple.

17 And He began to teach and say to them,

"Is it not written, 'My house shall be called a house of prayer for all the nations'? But you have made it a robbers' den."

18 The chief priests and the scribes heard this, and began seeking how to destroy Him; for they were afraid of Him, for the whole crowd was astonished at His teaching.

19 When evening came, they would go out of the city.

MARK 11:20–26

20 As they were passing by in the morning, they saw the fig tree withered from the roots up.

• Mark told us Jesus had walked through the temple when He entered Jerusalem the day before and looked at everything. What did He do in the temple on this day, and why?

THIS TEMPLE WAS VERY DIFFERENT AND WAS NOT RESPECTFUL.

• What did Jesus teach this day, and what was the response of the different people who heard Him?

FAITH / RESPECT FOR THE TEMPLE

OBSERVE

Leader: Read Mark 11:20–26 aloud. Have the group mark...

• *faith and believe(s) with an open book:* ⌐⌐

• *references to prayer, like this:* ⟨prayer⟩

• *forgive with a big* **X**.

DISCUSS

- What did the disciples notice as they passed the fig tree the next morning? How did Jesus use the withered fig tree as a teaching tool, and what was His message?

IT HAD WITHERED
HAVE FAITH IN GOD

- What do you learn from marking *faith* and *believe(s)*? *THEY WORK HAND IN HAND*

- What do you learn from marking references to prayer?

BELIEVE AND HAVE FAITH

- What difference does it make whether or not we forgive others?

IF YOU DO NOT FOREGIVE YOU WILL NOT BE FORGIVEN

- From what you learned about what was going on in the temple and the intent of the chief priests and the scribes in verse 18, did they deserve the blessing of God or the curse of God? Explain your answer.

THEY WERE MORE CONCERNED OF HOW THEY LOOKED IN THE EYES OF THE PEOPLE AND THEY DIDN'T LIKE JESUS GETTING ALL THE ATTENTION

21 Being reminded, Peter said to Him, "Rabbi, look, the fig tree which You cursed has withered."

22 And Jesus answered saying to them, "Have faith in God.

23 "Truly I say to you, whoever says to this mountain, 'Be taken up and cast into the sea,' and does not doubt in his heart, but believes that what he says is going to happen, it will be granted him.

24 "Therefore I say to you, all things for which you pray and ask, believe that you have received them, and they will be granted you.

25 "Whenever you stand praying, forgive, if you have anything against anyone, so that your Father who is in heaven will also forgive you your transgressions.

26 ["But if you do not forgive, neither will your Father who is in heaven forgive your transgressions."]

MARK 11:27–33

27 They came again to Jerusalem. And as He was walking in the temple, the chief priests and the scribes and the elders came to Him,

28 and began saying to Him, "By what authority are You doing these things, or who gave

• What comparison(s) could you draw between the fig tree and the hearts of the temple leaders?

NOT PRODUCING ANYTHING TO PLEASE JESUS

OBSERVE

Leader: *Read Mark 11:27–33 aloud and have the group…*
- *mark every reference to **Jesus**.*
- *double underline anything that indicates **location**, including **the temple**.*
- *put a big **A** over every occurrence of **authority**.*

INSIGHT

The Sanhedrin, a ruling body of seventy-one men presided over by the high priest, governed their people under the authority of Rome. Comprised of chief priests, teachers of the Law, and elders from the Saduccees and the Pharisees, the Sanhedrin was the council of authority in Jewish matters.

DISCUSS

• Who confronted Jesus when He returned to the temple? What did they ask?

CHEIF PRIESTS, SCRIBES AND ELDERS

WHY ARE YOU DOING THESE THINGS. BY WHOS AUTHORITY ?

You this authority to do these things?"

29 And Jesus said to them, "I will ask you one question, and you answer Me, and then I will tell you by what authority I do these things.

30 "Was the baptism of John from heaven, or from men? Answer Me."

31 They began reasoning among themselves, saying, "If we say, 'From heaven,' He will say, 'Then why did you not believe him?'

32 "But shall we say, 'From men'?"—they were afraid of the people, for everyone considered John to have been a real prophet.

³³ Answering Jesus, they said, "We do not know." And Jesus said to them, "Nor will I tell you by what authority I do these things."

MARK 12:1–12

¹ And He began to speak to them in parables: "A man planted a vineyard and put a wall around it, and dug a vat under the wine press and built a tower, and rented it out to vine-growers and went on a journey.

² "At the harvest time he sent a slave to the vine-growers, in order to receive some of the produce of the vineyard from the vine-growers.

• How did Jesus handle this confrontation? What can you learn from this about dealing with people who want to discredit you? *HE ASKED THEM A QUESTION TO DETERMINE THEIR FAITH.*

EXPOSE YOUR ADVISARY

OBSERVE

Apparently, Jesus was not finished with the chief priests, scribes, and elders who had questioned His authority. Let's see what else Jesus said to them.

Leader: Read Mark 12:1–12 aloud. Have the group…

• *mark every reference to **Jesus.***

• *underline every reference to **the man who plants a vineyard**, including pronouns and synonyms regarding the owner of the vineyard.*

• *number **the various encounters** between the vine-growers and the owner of the vineyard.*

DISCUSS

- What did you learn from marking the references to Jesus?

HE STOOD HIS GROUND AND CHALLENGED NON BELIEVERS

- What did you learn from marking references to the owner of the vineyard?

HE SENT OTHERS TO DO WHAT HE WANTED

INSIGHT

Religious Jews would be aware of Isaiah 5, where God describes the nation of Israel as His vineyard and warned about what He would do to His vineyard because of their rebellion and disobedience.

3 "They took him, and beat him and sent him away empty-handed.

4 "Again he sent them another slave, and they wounded him in the head, and treated him shamefully.

5 "And he sent another, and that one they killed; and so with many others, beating some and killing others.

6 "He had one more to send, a beloved son; he sent him last of all to them, saying, 'They will respect my son.'

7 "But those vine-growers said to one another, 'This is the heir; come, let us kill him, and the inheritance will be ours!'

8 "They took him, and killed him and threw him out of the vineyard.

9 "What will the owner of the vineyard do? He will come and destroy the vine-growers, and will give the vineyard to others.

10 "Have you not even read this Scripture: 'The stone which the builders rejected, this became the chief corner stone;

11 This came about from the LORD, and it is marvelous in our eyes'?"

12 And they were seeking to seize Him, and yet they feared the people, for they understood that He spoke the parable against them. And so they left Him and went away.

• Who does the beloved son in the parable represent? How can you tell?

JESUS AS HE DIED THAT OTHER'S MAY PROSPER

• And who is the rejected stone, and who is telling the parable?

JESUS

OBSERVE

The chief priests, scribes, and elders may have walked away, but they hadn't given up on their plan to discredit Jesus.

Leader: Read Mark 12:13–17 aloud and have the group...

- *mark **Pharisees** and **Herodians** with a big **P**.*
- *mark each mention of **Jesus**.*

DISCUSS

- What do you learn from marking *Pharisees* and *Herodians*?

EACH ONLY MENTIONED ONCE

- Did they really mean what they said about Jesus in verse 14? Explain your answer.

YES, I THINK THEY WERE ACKNOWLEDGING WHO HE WAS AND YET THEIR AGENDA WAS TO TRAP HIM.

MARK 12:13–17

13 Then they sent some of the Pharisees and Herodians to Him in order to trap Him in a statement.

14 They came and said to Him, "Teacher, we know that You are truthful and defer to no one; for You are not partial to any, but teach the way of God in truth. Is it lawful to pay a poll-tax to Caesar, or not?

15 "Shall we pay or shall we not pay?" But He, knowing their hypocrisy, said to them, "Why are you testing Me? Bring Me a denarius to look at."

16 They brought one. And He said to them,

"Whose likeness and inscription is this?" And they said to Him, "Caesar's."

17 And Jesus said to them, "Render to Caesar the things that are Caesar's, and to God the things that are God's." And they were amazed at Him.

Mark 12:18–27

18 Some Sadducees (who say that there is no resurrection) came to Jesus, and began questioning Him, saying,

19 "Teacher, Moses wrote for us that if a man's brother dies and leaves behind a wife and leaves no child, his brother should marry the wife and

• How did Jesus handle these men? How would you describe the nature of His response to them?

HE CHALLANGED THEM. MATTER OF FACT AND KINDA IN YOUR FACE YOUR DIGGING YOUR OWN HOLE.

OBSERVE

Leader: Read Mark 12:18–27 aloud. Have the group…

- *mark each reference to **Jesus.***
- *draw a tombstone over every reference to **dying**, like this:* ⌂
- *mark every reference to **resurrection** or **rising from the dead** with an upward arrow, like this:* ↑

DISCUSS

• What do you learn from marking the references to death and resurrection?

HE SPEAKS MORE OF DEATH THAN RESURRECTION

• According to Jesus in verse 24, what is the Sadducees' problem?

THEY ARE MISTAKEN AND DON'T UNDERSTAND THE SCRIPTURES AND THE POWER OF GOD.

• Where does Jesus take them to find the answer? What do you learn from verse 26?

THE BOOK OF MOSES

DON'T MESS WITH JESUS

raise up children to his brother.

20 "There were seven brothers; and the first took a wife, and died leaving no children.

21 "The second one married her, and died leaving behind no children; and the third likewise;

22 and so all seven left no children. Last of all the woman died also.

23 "In the resurrection, when they rise again, which one's wife will she be? For all seven had married her."

24 Jesus said to them, "Is this not the reason you are mistaken, that you do not understand the Scriptures or the power of God?

25 "For when they rise from the dead, they neither marry nor are given in marriage, but are like angels in heaven.

26 "But regarding the fact that the dead rise again, have you not read in the book of Moses, in the passage about the burning bush, how God spoke to him, saying, 'I am the GOD of Abraham, and the GOD of Isaac, and the GOD of Jacob'?

27 "He is not the God of the dead, but of the living; you are greatly mistaken."

• What did you learn about heaven from Jesus' words in verse 25?

EVERYONE IN HEAVEN WILL BE AN ANGEL BUT NO ONE WILL BE ATTACHED TO ANYONE

• What lesson, if any, do you find for us in Jesus' words in this passage?

WE WILL ALL BE THERE TO SERVE GOD

OBSERVE

Leader: Read Mark 12:28–34 aloud. Have the group do the following:

- *Mark each occurrence of **commandment**, and references to commandments such as **foremost** and **second**, like this:* ⌓
- *Mark **love** with a heart:* ♡
- *Circle each occurrence of the word* (**all.**)
- *Draw a box around **kingdom of God**:* ▭

DISCUSS

- What commandment is foremost of all?

WALKING WITH GoD
AS HE WOUlD HAVE YoU

- What does it mean to love with all your heart, soul, mind, and strength? What would that look like in daily living?

MARK 12:28–34

28 One of the scribes came and heard them arguing, and recognizing that He had answered them well, asked Him, "What commandment is the foremost of all?"

29 Jesus answered, "The foremost is, 'Hear, O Israel! The LORD our God is one LORD;

30 and you shall love the LORD your GOD with all your heart, and with all your soul, and with all your mind, and with all your strength.'

31 "The second is this, 'You shall love your neighbor as yourself.' There is no other

commandment greater than these."

32 The scribe said to Him, "Right, Teacher; You have truly stated that He is One, and there is no one else besides Him;

33 and to love Him with all the heart and with all the understanding and with all the strength, and to love one's neighbor as himself, is much more than all burnt offerings and sacrifices."

34 When Jesus saw that he had answered intelligently, He said to him, "You are not far from the kingdom of God." After that, no one would venture to ask Him any more questions.

• Are you loving God with your all?

NO, I FALL SHORT

• What is the second commandment, and how is it related to the first?

LOVE YOUR NEIGHBOR AS YOURSELF.

PUT NO ONE ABOVE GOD

• What do you do for God? What sacrifices do you make? What do you give for the work of ministry? Why? What is the essential motivation?

I TRY TO BE A DECIPLE NOT MANY AS I CAN PLEASING GOD IS PARAMONT

WRAP IT UP

Do you wonder about the connection between the entry of Jesus into Jerusalem and the parable of the vineyard owner finally sending his son? What did the tenants do to the son in the story? They killed him. Why? They wanted the vineyard for themselves.

Although the text of this lesson began with people shouting Hosanna to Jesus, the subsequent scenes lead us to anticipate His coming rejection. "The stone [Jesus] which the builders rejected, this became the chief corner stone" (Mark 12:10).

Loving is the opposite of rejecting. When asked about the greatest commandment, Jesus identified it as loving God. But how are we to love Him? Did you notice the tiny little word "all"? *All* of our heart, soul, mind, and strength is what God requires of our love toward Him.

How about you? As you listen to the words of Jesus, are you prompted to examine yourself? How much do you really love God? And how is that love evident in your life? We encourage you to think on these things and take them to God in prayer this week.

Directed by the Spirit of God, the Old Testament prophet Amos wrote that the Lord does nothing but what He told His prophets beforehand. God does not want us in the dark when it comes to the future.

Thus Jesus prepared His own for what was yet to come, drawing on words from the Law and the Prophets—words already familiar to them—to make His point.

Listen carefully to His words, beloved of God, as it will prepare you for the challenging days ahead. Remember Jesus is there for you in any and every crisis. You can live as more than a conqueror through Him who loves you (Romans 8:37–39).

OBSERVE

Yet again we find Jesus in the temple teaching. However, instead of answering questions, we find Jesus asking them. He wants the people to reason through their understanding of the Christ (Messiah).

Leader: Read Mark 12:35–37 aloud. Have the group...
- *mark all references to **Jesus.***
- *mark any reference to **teaching** with a big **T.***

MARK 12:35–37

35 And Jesus began to say, as He taught in the temple, "How is it that the scribes say that the Christ is the son of David?

36 "David himself said in the Holy Spirit, 'The LORD said to my LORD, "Sit at My right hand, until I put Your enemies beneath Your feet."'

37 "David himself calls Him 'Lord'; so in what sense is He his son?" And the large crowd enjoyed listening to Him.

DISCUSS

• Where was Jesus, and what was He teaching? *TEMPLE*

• In the light of all you've learned, why is this important?

• What did Jesus do to make His point? In other words, what was His source, and what can you learn from this when trying to explain truth? *GOD IS THE SOURCE*

• Read verse 36 and put a triangle over the first occurrence of *Lord* and any pronouns that refer to Him. Who is this? *GOD*

• According to verse 36, what did the Holy Spirit say through David about his Lord, the one who is being spoken to?

• Mark all references to Him including *Your* with a **C** for Christ. Who is this Lord you just marked? *JESUS*

• What question did Jesus pose in verse 37? What did He want His listeners to understand?

• Who is King David's Lord? Think about
it: Who was it the crowd enjoyed listening to and blind Bartimaeus identified as
the Son of David?

JESUS

OBSERVE

Leader: Read Mark 12:38–44 aloud. Have
the group do the following:
   • *Mark every reference to **Jesus.***
   • *Mark each mention of **scribes,** includ-*
     *ing the pronoun **who,** with a big **P.***
   • *Underline every reference to **the***
     widow.
   • *Put a box around the word **all.***

DISCUSS

• What warning did Jesus give in His
teaching in verses 38–40?

DO NOT FLOUNT YOUR
LIFE STATUS

• What were the scribes doing, and what
would be the ultimate result of this?

DRAWING ATTENTION
TO THEMSELVES

MARK 12:38–44

38 In His teaching
He was saying:
"Beware of the scribes
who like to walk
around in long robes,
and like respectful
greetings in the market
places,

39 and chief seats in
the synagogues and
places of honor at ban-
quets,

40 who devour wid-
ows' houses, and for
appearance's sake offer
long prayers; these will
receive greater con-
demnation."

41 And He sat down opposite the treasury, and began observing how the people were putting money into the treasury; and many rich people were putting in large sums.

42 A poor widow came and put in two small copper coins, which amount to a cent.

43 Calling His disciples to Him, He said to them, "Truly I say to you, this poor widow put in more than all the contributors to the treasury;

44 for they all put in out of their surplus, but she, out of her poverty, put in all she owned, all she had to live on."

• Have you ever been caught up in the kind of sin Jesus attributed to the scribes? What can we learn from these words of Jesus to help us resist that temptation?

BE HUMBLE NOT BOASTFUL

• What did Jesus do in verse 41?

OBSERVED

• What do you learn about the widow?

GAVE ALL

• How does your giving compare to the widow's? Do you simply give out of your surplus?

10% PLUS

• You've heard, but how would truly listening to these words of Jesus affect your perspective on giving to the work of God?

PROBABLY WON'T CHANGE

OBSERVE

We've come to the final chapter in our study of this portion of the gospel of Mark—a prophetic passage. (The remaining chapters are covered in a separate 40-Minute Study, *Jesus: Understanding His Death and Resurrection*.)

If you've never studied prophecy before or have only heard the teaching of others without studying it for yourself, keep in mind that all we want you to do is focus on the facts of this chapter.

Let's see what the Spirit of God led Mark to record from Jesus' conversation with His disciples.

Leader: Read Mark 13:1–13 aloud. Have the group…

- *mark **Jesus** as you've done since you began.*
- *underline the words **you** and **your**.*
- *circle every occurrence of **when**.*

MARK 13:1–13

1 As He was going out of the temple, one of His disciples said to Him, "Teacher, behold what wonderful stones and what wonderful buildings!"

2 And Jesus said to him, "Do you see these great buildings? Not one stone will be left upon another which will not be torn down."

3 As He was sitting on the Mount of Olives opposite the temple, Peter and James and John and Andrew were questioning Him privately,

4 "Tell us, when will these things be, and what will be the sign when all these

things are going to be fulfilled?"

5 And Jesus began to say to them, "See to it that no one misleads you.

6 "Many will come in My name, saying, 'I am He!' and will mislead many.

7 "When you hear of wars and rumors of wars, do not be frightened; those things must take place; but that is not yet the end.

8 "For nation will rise up against nation, and kingdom against kingdom; there will be earthquakes in various places; there will also be famines. These things are merely the beginning of birth pangs.

DISCUSS

• Where was Jesus leaving, and what precipitated His comment in verse 2?

LEAVING THE TEMPLE

• According to verses 3–4, where was Jesus, who was with Him, and what did they want to know? What does the phrase "these things" refer to?

MOUNT OF OLIVES
PETER, JAMES, JOHN, ANDREW
WHEN WILL ALL THESE THIN[G]
TAKE PLACE — THE END

• Beginning at verse 5, move through the text and note what you learn from marking *you* and *your*. Be sure to discuss the reason noted for each instruction Jesus gave.

9 "But be on your guard; for they will deliver you to the courts, and you will be flogged in the synagogues, and you will stand before governors and kings for My sake, as a testimony to them.

10 "The gospel must first be preached to all the nations.

11 "When they arrest you and hand you over, do not worry beforehand about what you are to say, but say whatever is given you in that hour; for it is not you who speak, but it is the Holy Spirit.

12 "Brother will betray brother to death, and a father his child; and children

will rise up against parents and have them put to death.

13 "You will be hated by all because of My name, but the one who endures to the end, he will be saved."

MARK 13:14–27

14 "But when you see the abomination of desolation standing where it should not be (let the reader understand), then those who are in Judea must flee to the mountains.

15 "The one who is on the housetop must not go down, or go in to get anything out of his house;

16 and the one who is in the field must not

• Whom was Jesus referring to as "you"? Is it just the four named in verse 3? Explain your answer and exactly who you believe is included in His instructions.

I THINK EVERY ONE OF US WILL BE TESTED

OBSERVE

Leader: *Read Mark 13:14–27 aloud and slowly. Have the group…*
- *circle every phrase that has to do with* **time,** *including* **when, then, after.**
- *underline every occurrence of* **you.**
- *mark the references to* **Jesus,** *including* **the Son of Man.**

Leader: *Read the text through slowly, one more time. Have the group…*
- *put a cloud around the reference to* **the coming of the Son of Man,** *like this:*
- *mark* **elect** *with a big* **E.**

DISCUSS

- Move through the text a few verses at a time and discuss what you learn from your markings.

- What do you learn from verses 14–19? Cover what is going to happen, what Jesus told His listeners they are to do, and why.

DISTRUCTION
FLEE TO THE MOUNTAINS
DO NOT RETURN TO GET
YOUR COAT

- What do you learn about the time of tribulation in verses 19–20?

SWIFT / DISTRUCTIVE

turn back to get his coat.

17 "But woe to those who are pregnant and to those who are nursing babies in those days!

18 "But pray that it may not happen in the winter.

19 "For those days will be a time of tribulation such as has not occurred since the beginning of the creation which God created until now, and never will.

20 "Unless the Lord had shortened those days, no life would have been saved; but for the sake of the elect, whom He chose, He shortened the days.

21 "And then if any-one says to you, 'Behold, here is the Christ'; or, 'Behold, He is there'; do not believe him;

22 for false Christs and false prophets will arise, and will show signs and wonders, in order to lead astray, if possible, the elect.

23 "But take heed; behold, I have told you everything in advance.

24 "But in those days, after that tribulation, the sun will be dark-ened and the moon will not give its light,

25 and the stars will be falling from heaven, and the powers that are in the heavens will be shaken.

• What instructions did Jesus give in verses 21–23?

BEWARE OF FALSE PROPHETS

• According to verses 24–27 what will hap-pen after the tribulation of those days?

NO SUN – NO MOON LIGHT
STARS WILL FALL
THE HEAVENS WILL BE
SHAKEN

• What do you learn from marking *elect*? According to verse 20, how did they get to be part of the elect?

THE BELIVERS

OBSERVE

Leader: Read Mark 13:28–37 aloud and once again, slowly. Have the group do the following:

- *Circle all references to **time**.*
- *Put a box around every use of the word **you**.*
- *Mark every reference to **Jesus**, including pronouns and synonyms that refer to Him.*
- *Put a check mark over every **admonition to be on the alert**: ✓*

26 "Then they will see the Son of Man coming in clouds with great power and glory.

27 "And then He will send forth the angels, and will gather together His elect from the four winds, from the farthest end of the earth to the farthest end of heaven."

MARK 13:28–37

28 "Now learn the parable from the fig tree: when its branch has already become tender and puts forth its leaves, you know that summer is near.

29 "Even so, you too, when you see these things happening, recognize that He is near, right at the door.

30 "Truly I say to you, this generation will not pass away until all these things take place.

31 "Heaven and earth will pass away, but My words will not pass away.

32 "But of that day or hour no one knows, not even the angels in heaven, nor the Son, but the Father alone.

33 "Take heed, keep on the alert; for you do not know when the appointed time will come.

34 "It is like a man away on a journey, who upon leaving his

DISCUSS

• What do you learn from marking *you?*

EVERYONE

• Summarize what Jesus wanted His listeners to know about the future and how He instructed them to prepare.

BE MINE FUL OF THE END OF DAYS -- BE READY.

• What you have just observed in Mark 13 may leave you with many questions, as prophecy passages often do.* Even so, what application, if any, can you find in these words of Jesus for your life today?

GET RIGHT WITH THE LORD AND WORK FOR HIM UNTIL HE CALLS

house and putting his slaves in charge, assigning to each one his task, also commanded the doorkeeper to stay on the alert.

35 "Therefore, be on the alert—for you do not know when the master of the house is coming, whether in the evening, at midnight, or when the rooster crows, or in the morning—

36 in case he should come suddenly and find you asleep.

37 "What I say to you I say to all, 'Be on the alert!'"

---

* If you would like to pursue the study of prophecy in a 40-Minute Study style, we highly recommend *Discovering What the Future Holds* by Kay Arthur and Dr. Georg Huber. If you want to go still deeper, consider our Precept courses on Daniel, 2 Thessalonians, and Revelation—in that order.

WRAP IT UP

Life can be so very frustrating. Frightening. Seemingly futile.

Unjust. Unfair. Unending.

Will things *never* change? Will there *forever* be wars, rumors of war? Calamity? Catastrophe? Inhumanity?

Oh no, the Son of Man will come with great power and glory to rule the world in righteousness and justice.

As you just read, His coming, though yet future, is certain. Jesus told you what will precede His return, so be on the alert.

Listen to Jesus—the Son of God, the Son of Man, the Son of David. Not one of His words will fail. He is the Word!

ABOUT KAY ARTHUR AND PRECEPT MINISTRIES INTERNATIONAL

KAY ARTHUR is known around the world as an international Bible teacher, author, conference speaker, and host of the national radio and television programs *Precepts for Life,* which reach a worldwide viewing audience of over ninety-four million. Recipient of the NRB Hall of Fame Award in 2011, Kay is a four-time Gold Medallion Award–winning author of more than one hundred books and Bible studies. She received an honorary doctorate from Tennessee Temple University.

Kay and her husband, Jack, founded Precept Ministries International in 1970 in Chattanooga, Tennessee, with a vision to establish people in God's Word. Today, the ministry has a worldwide outreach. In addition to inductive-study training workshops and thousands of small-group studies across America, PMI ministers in 180 countries with inductive Bible studies translated into more than seventy languages, discipling people by teaching them how to discover Truth for themselves.

ABOUT DAVID ARTHUR

DAVID ARTHUR serves as chief executive officer of Precept Ministries International. Having been mentored by his parents, Jack and Kay Arthur, in the value of inductive Bible study, he shares their passion for establishing people in God's Word.

Prior to his role at Precept, David worked in the business world with IBM and small businesses. Starting in 1999 David served for several years as a pastor in both the Presbyterian Church of America and the Associate Reformed Presbyterian Church. Just before coming to Precept, he was vice president with Generous Giving, working with givers and pastors. David is a passionate and gifted teacher of God's Word. He holds a bachelor's degree in organizational management from Covenant College and a master of arts in theological studies from Reformed Theological Seminary.

Contact Precept Ministries International for more information about inductive Bible studies in your area.

Precept Ministries International
PO Box 182218
Chattanooga, TN 37422-7218
800-763-8280
www.precept.org

40 MINUTE BIBLE STUDIES

No-Homework Bible Studies

That Help You Discover Truth For Yourself

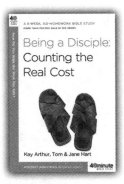

A 6-WEEK, NO-HOMEWORK BIBLE STUDY
MORE THAN 700,000 SOLD IN THE SERIES

Being a Disciple:
Counting the Real Cost

Kay Arthur, Tom & Jane Hart

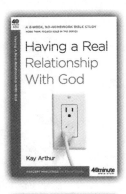

A 6-WEEK, NO-HOMEWORK BIBLE STUDY
MORE THAN 700,000 SOLD IN THE SERIES

Having a Real Relationship With God

Kay Arthur

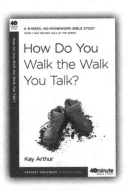

A 6-WEEK, NO-HOMEWORK BIBLE STUDY
MORE THAN 700,000 SOLD IN THE SERIES

How Do You Walk the Walk You Talk?

Kay Arthur

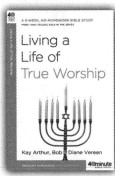

A 6-WEEK, NO-HOMEWORK BIBLE STUDY
MORE THAN 700,000 SOLD IN THE SERIES

Living a Life of True Worship

Kay Arthur, Bob & Diane Vereen

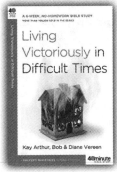

A 6-WEEK, NO-HOMEWORK BIBLE STUDY
MORE THAN 700,000 SOLD IN THE SERIES

Living Victoriously in Difficult Times

Kay Arthur, Bob & Diane Vereen

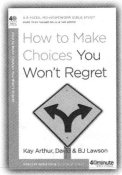

A 6-WEEK, NO-HOMEWORK BIBLE STUDY

How to Make Choices You Won't Regret

Kay Arthur, David & BJ Lawson

Money and Possessions: The Quest for Contentment

Kay Arthur & David Arthur

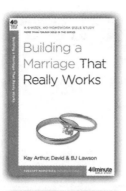

Building a Marriage That Really Works

Kay Arthur, David & BJ Lawson

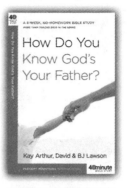

How Do You Know God's Your Father?

Kay Arthur, David & BJ Lawson

Discovering What the Future Holds

Kay Arthur & Georg Huber

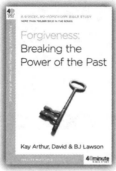

Forgiveness: Breaking the Power of the Past

Kay Arthur, David & BJ Lawson

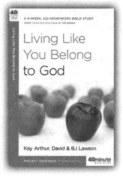

Living Like You Belong to God

Kay Arthur, David & BJ Lawson

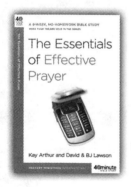

The Essentials of Effective Prayer

Kay Arthur and David & BJ Lawson

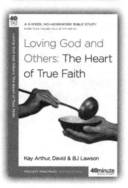

Loving God and Others: The Heart of True Faith

Kay Arthur, David & BJ Lawson

Understanding Spiritual Gifts

Kay Arthur, David and BJ Lawson

Also Available:

A Man's Strategy for
  Conquering Temptation
Rising to the Call of Leadership
Key Principles of Biblical Fasting
What Does the Bible Say About Sex?
Turning Your Heart Toward God

Fatal Distractions: Conquering
  Destructive Temptations
Spiritual Warfare: Overcoming the Enemy
The Power of Knowing God
Breaking Free from Fear
Finding Hope After Divorce

Another powerful study series
from beloved Bible teacher

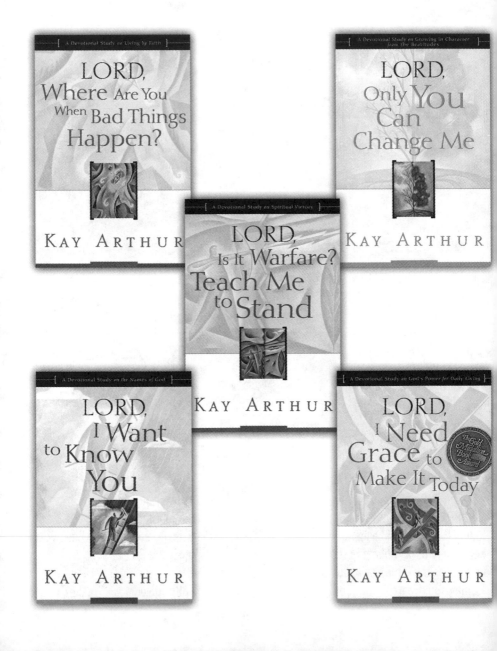

KAY ARTHUR

The Lord series provides insightful, warm-hearted Bible studies designed to meet you where you are—and help you discover God's answers to your deepest needs.

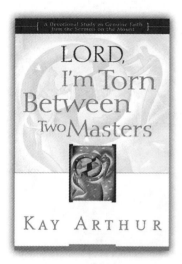

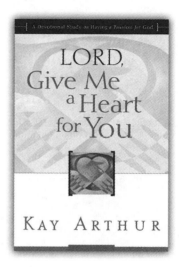

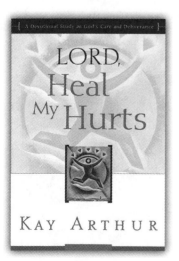

ALSO AVAILABLE:
One-year devotionals to draw you closer to the heart of God.